FIREFLIES

by Martha London

Consultant: Beth Gambro
Reading Specialist, Yorkville, Illinois

BEARPORT
PUBLISHING

Minneapolis, Minnesota

Teaching Tips

Before Reading

- Look at the cover of the book. Discuss the picture and the title.

- Ask readers to brainstorm a list of what they already know about fireflies. What can they expect to see in the book?

- Go on a picture walk, looking through the pictures to discuss vocabulary and make predictions about the text.

During Reading

- Read for purpose. As they are reading, encourage readers to think about the firefly's life and the impacts the bug has on other things.

- If readers encounter an unknown word, ask them to look at the sounds in the word. Then, ask them to look at the rest of the page. Are there any clues to help them understand?

After Reading

- Encourage readers to pick a buddy and reread the book together.

- Ask readers to name three things from the book that fireflies do. Go back and find the pages that tell about these things.

- Ask readers to write or draw something that they learned about fireflies.

Credits:
Cover and title page, © Fer Gregory / Shutterstock, © Brandon Alms / Shutterstock; 3, © TommyIX / iStock; 5, © Fer Gregory / Shutterstock; 6, © harmonia101 / iStock; 6, © moonisblack / iStock; 7, © Constantne / iStock; 8–9, © Ali Majdfar / gettyimages; 10–11, © Japan's Fireworks / Shutterstock; 12, © Petar Bogdanov / Shutterstock; 14–15, © zianlob / iStock; 17, © Gallinago_media / Shutterstock; 18, © Pally / Alamy; 21, © Shared Journey / Shutterstock; 22, © Andrew Darrington / Alamy,© Wirestock Creators / Shutterstock, © Andrew Newman Nature Pictures / Alamy, © hardcoreboy / iStock, © RichieChan / iStock; 23TL, © ABDESIGN / iStock; 23TR, © PointImages / iStock; 23BL, © Japan's Fireworks / Shutterstock; 23BR , © Terryfic3D / iStock.

Library of Congress Cataloging-in-Publication Data

Names: London, Martha, author.
Title: Fireflies / by Martha London.
Description: Bearcub books. | Minneapolis, Minnesota : Bearport Publishing Company, [2022] | Series: Bugs | Includes bibliographical references and index.
Identifiers: LCCN 2021026700 (print) | LCCN 2021026701 (ebook) | ISBN
  9781636913759 (library binding) | ISBN 9781636913827 (paperback) | ISBN
  9781636913896 (ebook)
Subjects: LCSH: Fireflies--Juvenile literature.
Classification: LCC QL596.L28 L66 2022 (print) | LCC QL596.L28 (ebook) |
  DDC 595.76/44--dc23
LC record available at https://lccn.loc.gov/2021026700
LC ebook record available at https://lccn.loc.gov/2021026701

For more information, write to Bearport Publishing, 5357 Penn Avenue South, Minneapolis, MN 55419. Printed in the United States of America.

Contents

Light Up the Night

Lights **flash** in the dark.

They go on and off.

And they zip here and there.

Fireflies bring light to the night.

5

There are many types of fireflies.

Most are black or brown.

Many are smaller than a paper clip.

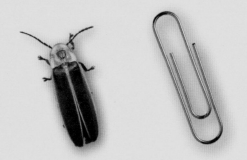

8

A lot of fireflies move around at night.

Some can make light.

Their bodies glow.

Firefly lights have two jobs.

They help the bugs see one another.

The lights also tell bigger animals fireflies taste bad.

Fireflies live in warm parts of the world.

They often stay near ponds or rivers.

The bugs do best in places that are warm and wet.

But fireflies are in **danger**.

People are harming land.

This hurts fireflies.

They need special places to live and have babies.

A baby firefly looks a little bit like a worm.

The baby crawls around.

Some baby fireflies even glow.

18

The baby eats other bugs.

The more it eats, the more it grows.

Soon, it turns into an **adult**.

It may grow wings and fly.

The adult moves from flower to flower.

It drinks sticky **nectar** from each.

Sip!

Most fireflies live for weeks or months.

A Firefly's Life

Egg

Larva

Pupa

Adult

Say larva
like LAHR-vuh

Say pupa
like PYOO-puh

Glossary

adult a grown-up

danger may be able to be hurt

flash to light up quickly

nectar a sticky liquid from flowers

Index

Read More

Davidson, Rose. *Glowing Animals (National Geographic Readers).* Washington, D.C.: National Geographic Kids, 2019.

Leaf, Christina. *Fireflies (Insects up Close).* Minneapolis: Bellwether Media, 2018.

Learn More Online

1. Go to **www.factsurfer.com** or scan the QR code below.
2. Enter "**Firefly Bug**" into the search box.
3. Click on the cover of this book to see a list of websites.

About the Author

Martha London lives in Minnesota with her cat. She has written more than 100 books for young readers!